RAI   CUE

KENYON, Linda

Rainforest bird
rescue

RAINFOREST BIRD RESCUE

Changing the Future for Endangered Wildlife

LINDA KENYON

FIREFLY BOOKS

A FIREFLY BOOK

Published by Firefly Books Ltd. 2006

First printing

PUBLISHER CATALOGUING-IN-PUBLICATION DATA (U.S.)
(Library of Congress Standards)

Kenyon, Linda.
Rainforest Bird rescue : changing the future for endangered wildlife / Linda Kenyon.
[64] p. : col. photos. ; cm. (Firefly animal rescue)
Includes index.
Summary: Provides details and facts about rainforest birds from around the world, their endangerment and a range of conservation programs to save them, including profiles of individual conservationists and rainforest bird species.
ISBN-10: 1-55407-153-4 — ISBN-13: 978-1-55407-153-1
ISBN-10: 1-55407-152-6 — ISBN-13: 978-1-55407-152-4 (pbk.)
1. Forest birds—Juvenile literature. 2. Rain forest animals—Juvenile literature. 3. Endangered species—Juvenile literature.
4. Wildlife conservation—Juvenile literature. I. Title. II. Series.
598.1734 dc22 QL676.2.K46 2006

LIBRARY AND ARCHIVES CANADA CATALOGUING IN PUBLICATION DATA
Kenyon, Linda
Rainforest bird rescue : changing the future for endangered wildlife / Linda Kenyon.
(Firefly animal rescue)
Includes index.
ISBN-10: 1-55407-153-4 — ISBN-13: 978-1-55407-153-1 (bound)
ISBN-10: 1-55407-152-6 — ISBN-13: 978-1-55407-152-4 (pbk.)
1. Forest birds—Juvenile literature. 2. Rain forest animals—Juvenile literature. 3. Endangered species—Juvenile literature.
4. Wildlife conservation—Juvenile literature. I. Title. II. Series.
QL695.5.K45 2006   j598.1734   C2005-907373-X

Published in the United States by
Firefly Books (U.S.) Inc.
P.O. Box 1338, Ellicott Station
Buffalo, New York 14205

Published in Canada by
Firefly Books Ltd.
66 Leek Crescent
Richmond Hill, Ontario L4B 1H1

nd interior design: Kathe Gray/electric pear and Ingrid Paulson

Printed in China

The publisher gratefully acknowledges the financial support for our publishing program by the Canada Council for the Arts, the Ontario Arts Council and the Government of Canada through the Book Publishing Industry Development Program.

TABLE OF CONTENTS

A SHRINKING PARADISE

Rainforests are a paradise for birds—moderate temperatures, lots of fruits and insects to eat. There's shelter from predators, and places to perch for those who are predators themselves. No wonder about a third of the world's bird species live in rainforests.

But all is not well for rainforest birds. In the last two centuries, more than a hundred bird species around the world have become extinct. Right now, almost 1,200 others—one in eight—are threatened with extinction. More than 700 of these are rainforest birds. Without our help, hundreds of rainforest bird species will disappear by the year 2100.

The main threat to rainforest birds is loss of habitat. A few thousand years ago, tropical rainforests covered as much as 12 percent of the earth's land surface. Today, that figure has been reduced by half.

Logging accounts for much of the loss—humans have an almost insatiable need for wood. We use it to make paper, to build houses, to furnish them, to heat them. Rainforests, with their thick stands of trees, are particularly attractive to logging companies. There are riches under the rainforest floor as well. The mining of natural gas, oil and minerals destroys vast areas of rainforest every year.

With logging and mining comes human settlement. Communities quickly spring up along newly built roads, and before long, people clear areas of the forest for building material and firewood, and to make way for crops and pastures. With people come invasive species such as cats and rats, which can take a heavy toll on rainforest birds.

The birds themselves become easy prey for hungry settlers. They are also trapped and sold as pets— one bird can bring in as much money as a farmer might make in six months. No wonder millions of rainforest birds find their way to pet stores every year. Many are threatened with extinction as a result.

Fortunately, people around the world are fighting to prevent the further extinction of even one more species of rainforest bird.

< The purple-throated mountain-gem, a hummingbird native to Costa Rica, is just one of thousands of bird species that make their home in rainforests.

WHERE DO RAINFOREST BIRDS LIVE?

Rainforest birds are found in both ·
tropical and temperate rainforests.

 tropical rainforest

temperate rainforest

THE STORY SO FAR

∧ Conservationists with BirdLife International and World Wildlife Fund scan the Indonesian rainforest for threatened birds.

In the past few decades, rainforests have fallen with alarming speed, but loss of habitat has not been the only threat.

1889 The Royal Society for the Protection of Birds is established in the United Kingdom to counter the trade in grebe feathers, used as a fur substitute in ladies' fashions. The RSPB has become one of the world's most influential conservation organizations, with more than a million members.

1922 The International Council for Bird Preservation (ICBP) is founded in London, England. Renamed BirdLife International in 1994, the council works in more than a hundred countries and is the leading authority on the status of birds and their habitats.

1951 The Alagoas curassow, a bird not seen in the wild since the mid-1600s, is rediscovered in El Salvador. As few as 20 individuals survive in the wild today.

1970s Central American coffee farmers begin using "sun cultivation" techniques that result in the destruction of millions of acres of forest.

1975 Eighteen countries agree to the Convention on International Trade in Endangered Species (CITES), which now protects some 1,700 species of bird. Since it came into force, not one of these species has become extinct as a result of trade.

1990 Studies reveal that one fifth of the world's tropical forest cover has been cleared since 1960—more than 1.5 million square miles (4 million km²).

An illegally imported African grey parrot is held at a shelter in Moscow, Russia. The CITES agreement now protects 1,700 birds—including almost all parrot species—from illegal trade.

1999 Home Depot announces its plan to stop selling wood products from environmentally sensitive areas.

2002 Brazil loses 9,840 square miles (25,000 km²) of its Amazon rainforest, 40 percent more than in 2001.

2003 Satellite and aerial photographs reveal that the Kilum-Ijim forest in Cameroon, West Africa, is recovering rapidly as a result of conservation efforts; Gurney's pitta is spotted for the first time in 89 years in Myanmar (Burma).

2004 A new species of rainforest bird, the flightless Calayan rail, is discovered on a remote island in the northern Philippines. In Costa Rica, Amigos de las Aves celebrates its first wild-breeding success: two juvenile birds are observed flying with a group of 13 captive-bred scarlet macaws that had been released in 1999.

2005 The Seychelles magpie-robin population recovers enough to be removed from the critically endangered list, though it is still classified as endangered.

IT'S A JUNGLE OUT THERE

Any forest that receives more than 78 inches (198 cm) of rain annually is generally considered a *rainforest*.

Tropical rainforests are located less than 22.5° north or south of the equator—between the Tropic of Capricorn and the Tropic of Cancer. The largest unbroken stretch of tropical rainforest is in the Amazon River basin in South America. More than half of this region is in Brazil, home to 30 percent of the world's remaining tropical rainforests. Another 20 percent is in Indonesia and the Congo Basin in Africa.

^ The Minnamurra rainforest of New South Wales, Australia, is an example of a temperate rainforest, which has a more moderate climate than its tropical counterpart.

Temperate rainforests also have high rainfall, but occur in regions with more mild or moderate climates, usually in places where sea air meets coastal mountains. Temperate rainforests are found in parts of Southern Australia, New Zealand, Chile, the United States, and Canada.

Rainforests are home to more than half the world's plant and animal species. A typical 4-square-mile (10.5 km²) patch of tropical rainforest contains up to 125 mammal species, 400 birds, 100 reptiles, 60 amphibians, and 150 butterflies. These living things have been evolving together for millions of years, and the loss of even one species threatens the survival of others.

Among rainforest plants, there is intense competition for sunlight. High above the forest floor, the crowns of tall, broad-leaved trees form a dense canopy. Occasional individual trees, known as emergents, rise beyond the canopy, sometimes to 200 feet (60 m). Below the canopy are two or three levels of shade-tolerant trees, such as palms. The entire forest is laced together by a network of vines called lianas.

In a Peruvian rainforest, a harpy eagle looks down from an emergent tree. Emergents rise well above the canopy and are a favorite nesting and perching site for birds of prey.

Most animals have adapted to life in a particular part of the rainforest. Eagles, for example, are most at home in the emergent trees, where they keep a sharp eye out for prey in the trees below. Monkeys, flying squirrels, and sharp-clawed woodpeckers inhabit the treetops, rarely coming down to ground level. Large mammals such as elephants, deer and leopards wander the forest floor, which is overflowing with insect life.

There's much we still don't know about rainforest life—only a small number of species have been discovered. But there's one thing we do know: rainforests and the creatures that inhabit them don't tolerate disturbance.

CROWD CONTROL

There are about 6.5 billion human beings in the world today, and that number is increasing by the minute. In the time it takes you to read this page, the number of people on earth will increase by about 140.

That's a lot of people. And all those people need a place to live, which can be bad news for birds. When the needs of humans and the needs of birds come into conflict, the birds rarely win. Rainforests are being cleared at an alarming rate, with little or no thought given to where the birds will go.

Even when the trees are left standing, human settlements can have a devastating effect on birds. When land is cleared around a forest to make way for houses, predators suddenly have easy access to the forest interior. These include not just wild animals like foxes and raccoons, but cats and dogs as well. Even escaped pet birds can wreak havoc with forest species. Towns and villages usually attract rats, which are notorious nest robbers. Finally, household chemicals, fertilizers and pesticides can harm and even kill forest birds.

< An aerial photograph of a Brazilian river dramatically shows the effect of deforestation—one bank is covered by dense rainforest, while the other has been cleared for farmland.

PLEASE DON'T EAT THE CURASSOWS

∧ A boat tows a load of illegal timber on the Amazon. Logging and other habitat destruction is responsible for the decline of the wattled curassow.

More than a billion people in the tropics live in absolute poverty. With poverty comes hunger, and when you're really hungry, even a wattled curassow looks good.

The wattled curassow (*Crax globulosa*) is a conspicuous creature. The male has a bright red knob on top of its bill and a round wattle, like on a turkey, underneath it. It perches in trees along rivers in the rainforest, and forages for food in groups on the forest floor, making it an easy target for hunters who are simply trying to feed themselves and their families. Once widespread in forests along the Amazon river, it is declining rapidly. The introduction of shotguns by European settlers had a serious effect on the bird, which was previously hunted by blowguns or trapped.

But local people aren't solely responsible for the decline of the wattled curassow. It also suffers from the same threat as many other rainforest birds: habitat destruction. The world's demand for fur coats, rubber and mahogany furniture has led to more and more people venturing into the once remote areas where the wattled curassow lives, increasing the bird's exposure to one of the deadliest predators: humans.

Similar to a turkey in its facial appearance, the male wattled curassow has prominent knobs of red flesh above and below its bill.

A temporary hunting ban in Bolivia, one of a handful of places in South America where the bird remains, has made a small contribution to its recovery. The local community is also gaining more awareness of the bird's plight through public presentations and the distribution of shirts with a colorful picture of a pair of Mamaco, as the locals call curassows. On the back of the shirts are the words of the community elders:

> I don't hunt Mamaco
> There were many
> Now there are almost none
> In all of Bolivia
> In all of South America
> Let it return

The Kilum-Ijim Forest Project is one of those rare things: a rainforest story with a happy ending. Or at least hope for a happy ending, as the story isn't over yet.

∧ Cameroonians erect a sign to let local people know of the conservation project in their forest. A supportive community is the main reason for the project's success.

Twenty years ago, things didn't look good. Located in western Cameroon, one of the most densely populated areas in West Africa, the Kilum-Ijim forest was being cleared to grow crops and graze livestock by the 200,000 people who live within a day's walk of the area. In 1992, conservationists estimated that if things continued, the entire forest would disappear within five years.

Fortunately, BirdLife International was already on the scene. The organization began working in the area in 1987, and its first goal was to put a stop to the clearing. Today, satellite photos show that the forest is recovering. Why has this project succeeded where others have not? Because it has involved the people who live near the forest, rather than trying to impose rules from the outside. And because it has found sustainable ways for the community to benefit.

The project received some unexpected help from a large, dark green bird with a distinctive orange crest and bright red feathers on the underside of its wings. The Kilum-Ijim forest is the last remaining home of Bannerman's turaco (*Tauraco bannermani*), a bird of great cultural importance to Cameroon's Kom people. A mask resembling the colorful bird is worn in an important ceremonial dance, and its red feathers are given by chiefs as a reward for service.

"People don't necessarily realize that the birds they've known all their lives don't exist elsewhere," says Jonathan Barnard of BirdLife. "But once they do know, it adds to their motivation to protect their forest."

Bannerman's turaco feeds on fruit that grows high in the forest canopy, and it can survive as long as some tall fruit trees remain. But there's a limit to what the bird can tolerate. When cattle graze in the forest, they create open patches in the canopy, and the birds don't like to fly across these spaces. Fires create even larger gaps in the forest.

To protect both the endangered bird and their own livelihood, local people suggested even stricter rules for protecting the forest than conservationists expected. They willingly participated in a program to help them make the best use of crop and grazing land, and were eager to learn about other uses of the forest such as beekeeping, papermaking and wood carving. They're also exploring ecotourism as another way of earning money.

"Most people have a great pride in their forest," says Barnard. "But they also have to live, and if they get direct financial benefits from the forest, they put even greater efforts into protecting it."

^ (top) The Kilum-Ijim forest is the last remaining home of Bannerman's turaco. (bottom) Kom people wear masks resembling the bird during an important dance ritual.

THE COMFORTS OF HOME

Look around your home. What would it be like without a kitchen table, books and magazines, frames around the windows and doors? Now think about what it would be like if you didn't have a home at all—that's the situation many rainforest birds now face because of the human appetite for wood.

In many poor countries, governments have little choice but to sell logging and mining rights to companies in order to pay off huge debts. Many of these companies have little concern for the future—sometimes they simply clear-cut the forest to maximize their profit. Even when they cut only selected trees, vines often pull down surrounding ones, leaving gaping holes. These expose the forest floor to sunlight, drying it up and reducing the number of insects that birds feed on.

All of this is bad news for rainforest birds like the newly discovered Calayan rail (*Gallirallus calayanensis*). Found only on a remote island in the northern Philippines, the dark brown bird rummages for food on the rainforest floor, turning over dried leaves and other debris with its bright red bill. The bird is flightless, making it more vulnerable to hunters and predators such as cats and rats—in fact, 18 of the 20 species of flightless rail are considered threatened.

Fortunately, some big buyers of wood products, such as Home Depot, are doing what they can to take the pressure off rainforests. In 1999, the company began giving preference to wood that has come from forests managed in a responsible way. Home Depot has also pledged not to purchase wood products from the world's endangered forests, including those in the Philippines, where the Calayan rail makes its home.

< Flightless birds such as the Calayan rail—not discovered by scientists until May 2004—are especially vulnerable to predators. They require large areas of undisturbed forest to survive.

BURIED RICHES

Rainforests often lie on rich natural gas, oil and mineral deposits, and the extraction of these valuable resources degrades or destroys bird habitat.

^ Oil spills can contaminate acres of rainforest by seeping into the groundwater.

What harm can an oil well do to acres of rainforest? Plenty. Clearing the forest to drill a well is often just the start of the problem. Spills can contaminate the water and soil, and often the shortest route from a well to a refinery is through fragile habitat. Sometimes oil companies burn natural gas in the open air, a process known as flaring. This causes air pollution and fires that destroy acres of forest and threaten the lives of birds and other animals—not to mention local people.

Mining is another serious threat to the world's rainforests. Gold mining companies, for example, dig enormous pits and use dynamite to blast holes in the ground, disturbing birds for miles around. The companies also use cyanide to help extract the gold, and this toxic chemical can poison streams and rivers.

On Christmas Island, near Indonesia, phosphate mining has had a devastating effect on Abbott's booby (*Papasula abbotti*), a large seabird with a white body and black wings. The birds spend a lot of time in their nests, which they make in emergent trees, so many adults and young birds were killed when these trees were cut down for mines. Gaps in the forest also increase wind turbulence, making it harder for the birds to land, and since they cannot take off from the ground, they may starve if they fall into a cleared area. Scientists have noted a sharp increase in the death rate of adult and fledgling birds around the edges of clearings.

24

Some seabirds, such as Abbott's booby, nest only in tall, emergent rainforest trees. On Christmas Island, clearing the forest for mining has led to the loss of many nesting trees.

Today, most remaining Abbott's booby habitat is protected within the Christmas Island National Park. Mining companies are not allowed to clear primary rainforest, and they must help pay to plant trees around the bird's nesting sites to act as a wind break.

Perhaps the species will have a smooth landing after all.

A small, round-faced owl with chocolate brown eyes may not be the first thing that comes to mind when you think "rainforest bird." The northern spotted owl (*Strix occidentalis caurina*) is indeed one of Canada's few rainforest birds—and one of the country's most endangered species.

^ The northern spotted owl, one of Canada's few rainforest birds, needs up to 20 square miles of old-growth forest per breeding pair.

Though the owls were once common, scientists estimate that as few as 25 pairs remain in the ancient rainforests of British Columbia. Because they nest in cavities of old trees, they can survive only in mature forests, where they can find plenty of flying squirrels, their favorite food. The dense, closed canopy provides them with protection from their chief predators, northern goshawks and great horned owls.

Northern spotted owls need up to 20 square miles (52 km²) of ancient forest per breeding pair, and that's becoming hard to find in British Columbia, where logging of old-growth forests is big business.

In 2002, the Western Canada Wilderness Committee showed that the decline of the spotted owl was linked to logging. The environmental group didn't shy away from naming names, and it has since taken several companies to court to stop them from logging in spotted owl habitat.

But their efforts go well beyond the courtroom. In May 2004, the group organized a two-day camp-out to bring public attention to the clear-cutting of a forest near Hope, British Columbia. They also set up a semi-permanent camp in the park and hung banners over the highway protesting the logging of this known spotted owl habitat.

Dressed as owls to call attention to a threatened bird species, Greenpeace activists demonstrate against the clear-cutting of ancient North American rainforests.

"Sadly, however, the logging continued," says Joe Foy, a spokesman for the group. He doesn't hold much hope for the species in Canada. "This country has so few spotted owls remaining that they will likely disappear from the landscape sometime before the 2010 Winter Olympics," which are to be held in the Vancouver-Whistler region of southwest B.C.—the heart of spotted owl territory.

Still, the Western Canada Wilderness Committee will continue its fight to preserve the owl's remaining habitat. "This fight is the same for many species around the planet," says Foy. "I have to believe that many of these fights will eventually be won."

Most days, the posters on her office walls are as close as Neva Murtha gets to a rainforest. Yet she does as much for the ancient forests of the world as people who spend every minute of the day in them.

Murtha works for Greenpeace in downtown Vancouver, and it's her job to persuade book and magazine publishers to use paper that comes from sustainable sources. Paper is still often made from British Columbia's ancient rainforest trees, but people like Murtha are encouraging publishers to use recycled paper, or paper made from plant fibers such as hemp or straw. Most of these products are more expensive, but Murtha says that will change. "Once enough publishers demand environmentally friendly papers, mills will have an incentive to develop them." In time, Greenpeace and its partners hope to convince Canadian publishers to switch entirely to "ancient-forest friendly" paper.

^ Neva Murtha works hard to convince publishers to use paper from sustainable sources.

Murtha first witnessed the devastating effects of logging as a teenager, when she flew over northern Vancouver Island with her father, a forestry professor. "I remember seeing the clear-cuts and thinking that there was important work to be done to protect these forests and the creatures that live in them."

Today, Murtha is working hard to protect the old-growth forests that remain. "These ancient forests are such rich ecosystems, supporting so much life." She's hopeful about the future of these forests, though she's concerned about people's understanding of their importance. "Ancient forests know how to take care of themselves. They have developed over 10,000 years in harmony with the humans who inhabited them, until the last 100 to 150 years. As long as people remain unaware that their paper and lumber demands are harming the world's last ancient forests, the forests are at risk."

< Clear-cutting in British Columbia, the heart of northern spotted owl territory. Until the public changes its demands for wood products, the harvesting of forests will continue.

BIRDS WITHOUT BORDERS

A Victoria crowned pigeon (*Goura victoria*) foraging on the forest floor spots an interesting pile of leaf litter a few feet away and takes a couple of steps to the west. The bird doesn't know it, but its life is now in danger. It has just left Papua New Guinea—the eastern half of the Pacific island of New Guinea, where the pigeon is protected by law—and entered Indonesian territory, where it's fair game for hunters. The bird is prized for its meat, and is so easy to catch because of its gentle, curious nature that it survives only deep in the forest, far from humans.

∧ The cerulean warbler has to survive many hazards during its 4,500 mile migration.

Whether they spend most of their time on the ground or in the air, all birds move from place to place without regard for political borders. That's why they can be so hard to protect. Birds that range widely risk wandering into unprotected or even hostile territory. On longer journeys they can fall victim to predators, bad weather or a lack of water or food.

People don't usually think of rainforest birds as migratory, but some species travel thousands of miles in a year. The cerulean warbler (*Dendroica cerulea*), for example, winters in the forests of South America and flies as many as 4,500 miles (7,250 km) to nest in Canada.

Gathering data on species that range so freely, deciding how to protect them and getting countries to cooperate can be a challenge. But there have been some positive signs. In the last two decades, the Convention on Migratory Species has been signed by 85 countries in Africa, Central and South America, Asia, Europe, and the Pacific islands. The agreement requires governments to work together to protect threatened species that migrate across borders.

The Victoria crowned pigeon, named for its spectacular head ornament, is much prized for its meat.   >

ATTACK OF THE CRAZY ANTS

Rhinoceros hornbills (*Buceros rhinoceros*) have developed an elaborate strategy for keeping snakes and other enemies out of their nests. Using material that she scrapes from the inside of the nest hole, the female seals herself into a tree cavity, leaving just a small opening through which the male passes food. When the chicks are seven weeks old, the female breaks out of the nest and the chicks reseal the entrance. Both the male and the female continue to feed the chicks until they are ready to leave the nest.

^ Yellow crazy ants attack a land crab. The marauding insects have also driven birds from their nests.

Like the rhinoceros hornbill, many rainforest birds are amazingly well defended against natural predators. But they can be helpless in the face of unfamiliar species. When forests are logged, or cleared for farming or to build homes, predators move in. Domestic cats take a terrible toll on rainforest birds. So do rats and insects, which people may introduce unknowingly.

On Christmas Island, northwest of Australia, yellow crazy ants (named for their frantic movements) seriously threatened bird populations. Accidentally brought to the island more than 70 years ago, these ants became a problem when, for some reason, they suddenly began forming "supercolonies" that covered hundreds of acres. The ants forage mainly in the rainforest canopy and in these huge numbers are capable of driving birds from their nests.

The rhinoceros hornbill is helpless in the face of alien species, which can alter the structure of a rainforest.

Perhaps more seriously, the ants had begun to alter the structure of the forest itself by killing off red land crabs, which feed along the forest floor. More seeds began to germinate and the forest had begun to change dramatically.

Fortunately, a poisonous bait has brought the crazy ant problem under control, but it will be a while before the forest recovers.

When you live on an island in the middle of the Indian Ocean, you can't run away from your problems. Or fly away, in the case of the Seychelles magpie-robin (*Copsychus sechellarum*).

^ A researcher collects a blood sample from an immature Seychelles magpie-robin.

So when people began settling the islands in 1770, the birds had no place to go. It wasn't just that settlers cleared much of the forest, but they brought with them rats, cats, and mynah birds. Until the settlers arrived, the Seychelles magpie-robin had few natural predators, just native birds and lizards that occasionally ate eggs and chicks. Now the rats and mynah birds found the eggs and chicks of the Seychelles magpie-robin easy pickings. And the adult birds, which rummage for insects in leaf litter on the forest floor, were preyed on by cats.

Once found on at least six islands in the Seychelles, in the mid-1960s the species was reduced to just 12 to 15 birds on one island. It looked like the end, but they managed to hang on. Their numbers rose and fell over the next two decades and had dwindled again to around 20 birds when the Seychelles Magpie-Robin Recovery Program was established in 1990.

Once down to fewer than 20 birds, the Seychelles magpie-robin is now off the critical list.

The program put an end to a chemical people had been using to kill cockroaches—the pesticide also killed Seychelles magpie-robins that fed on the roaches. In addition, conservationists provided safe nest boxes to protect eggs and chicks and gave the birds extra food daily. Slowly, the numbers began to rise. But then in 1995, the birds suffered another setback: brown rats were accidentally brought to the island. Five years later, the rats were eliminated with poison and the birds continued to recover. Some were taken to other islands, and by 2005 the population had grown to 150 birds on four islands.

> "Their numbers are still increasing," says Rachel Bristol of Nature Seychelles. So much so that the bird was recently taken off the critically endangered list. There's still a long road ahead, but things are looking up. It proves that with some hard work, you can save the neighborhood.

VICTIMS OF FASHION

^ A spectator at the Royal Ascot horse races in Britain wears a hat decorated with a tropical bird feather.

Birds have one thing that distinguishes them from all other animals: feathers.

Feathers probably evolved from the scales of birds' reptile ancestors, and they serve many purposes. Birds are the best fliers in the world—better than insects or bats—thanks to their feathers. Feathers act as insulation, keeping birds warm in even the coldest water, and serve as camouflage, helping a nesting bird avoid detection by predators, for example. They are also important for display—the plumage of male birds, often more brilliant and patterned than that of females, attracts mates and warns off competitors, even predators.

Over the years the brilliant plumage of birds has attracted more than just the attention of other birds. Feathers have been used by people all over the world—in hats and headdresses, to make fans, arrows, fishing lures, pillows, quills for writing and many other items.

Our fascination with feathers has contributed to the decline of many birds. The now-endangered banded cotinga (*Cotinga maculata*), for example, was collected by people in Brazil for use in crafts. Though these striking birds are now confined to just a few protected areas in southeast Brazil, their blue feathers are still for sale on the Internet, where people buy them to make fishing lures.

These illegally exported parrot-feather ornaments were confiscated at the U.S. border.

Even one of the world's largest and most powerful birds of prey, the harpy eagle (*Harpia harpyja*) of South and Central America, is threatened by our desire for feathers. The eagle is an easy target because of its large size and boldness, and hunting is the most significant threat to this majestic bird. Its feathers are prized as symbols of power, and are coveted by local shamans and tourists alike.

43

HOW MUCH IS THAT PARROT IN THE WINDOW?

Have you ever looked at a caged parrot and thought it would make a great pet? You don't have to walk it, you only have to feed it daily and clean its cage once a week. Parrots look exotic. You can even teach them to talk.

You're not alone. Birds are the third most popular pet in the world, after cats and dogs. Unfortunately, when you look at a bird in a pet shop, it's difficult to know for sure whether it was bred in captivity or captured in the wild. People who buy wild-caught birds, even unknowingly, are taking part in a trade that is threatening the survival of many species.

More than 2,600 species—that's several million individual birds—are bought and sold each year. According to Animal Aid, the UK's largest animal rights group, 88 percent of parakeets, lovebirds, and related species imported into the UK between 1995 and 2000 were wild-caught.

How birds are trapped varies, but generally smaller ones are trapped in bulk and larger birds are captured individually. Small birds such as finches are caught in fine nets. If these are not checked often, the birds can struggle until they die of exhaustion or dehydration, if they're not eaten by predators first. Larger birds are snared or caught in baited cages, where they too can wait hours, even days, to be released. Even more cruel is the use of bird lime, a sticky substance applied to bushes and trees. Birds caught this way can lose many feathers in their struggle to free themselves.

< Parrots for the pet trade — like this yellow-headed amazon — may be snared, captured in baited cages, or trapped in bird lime, a sticky substance applied to bushes and trees.

Captured birds, like these in a Thailand marketplace, can spend weeks in overcrowded conditions before making their way to pet dealers around the world.

Once they've been trapped, the birds are transferred into baskets, boxes or bags and taken to the trapper's home, where they can stay for weeks or months in overcrowded conditions, often without enough food, water or light. Those that survive are flown to dealers and pet stores around the world. They don't all make it—for every bird bought as a pet, up to three others will have died during capture, in transit, or even in the pet shop.

Not surprisingly, many rare parrots are threatened because they're trapped for the bird trade. Some, such as the yellow-crested cockatoo of Indonesia and East Timor, are close to extinction. Others, such as Spix's macaw in Brazil, may already be extinct.

Conservationists are doing their best to control the trade in endangered birds. More than 160 countries have signed the Convention on International Trade in Endangered Species (CITES), a set of rules that aims to ensure that trade in wild animals and plants does not threaten their survival.

The illegal trade in wild birds may never stop unless the underlying causes are addressed. Poverty is a big one. Yellow-headed amazons sell for US$800 to $1,500, while a hyacinth macaw can fetch up to US$12,000, partly because only 2,000 to 5,000 remain in the wild. Though the person who actually traps one of these birds gets only a fraction of this amount, the money they make can equal six months' salary in some areas. Unless we find a way to do something about poverty in the countries these birds call home, the trade will continue.

∧ A sign in Costa Rica instructs people not to buy parrots from those who steal them from their nests.

47

For many people, Sunday is a day of rest. Not so for Richard and Margot Frisius. It's the busiest day of the week for the founders of Amigos de las Aves (Spanish for "Friends of the Birds") in Costa Rica. Their one employee has the day off, which leaves the couple with more than 100 scarlet macaws (*Ara macao*) and 50 great green macaws (*Ara ambigua*) to feed and care for. "And two little ducks and a small woodpecker that fell out of a tree," adds Margot.

∧ Richard and Margot Frisius are devoted to breeding macaws and introducing them into the wild.

People bring them rescued birds of many species, but their main focus is breeding Costa Rican macaws in order to introduce them into the wild. "The scarlets are doing quite well," Margot says. "There is a wild population of around 600 birds in two different areas." But the species remains under constant threat. The attractive scarlet, yellow and blue birds are highly sought after for the pet trade.

In 1999, Richard and Margot released their first flock of captive-bred scarlet macaws into a private wildlife refuge in Costa Rica. "It's nerve-racking letting them go," says Margot, who worries that the birds may be captured. "This is a developing country. A bird will bring six months' salary."

It took the birds a while to adjust to their new-found freedom. At first they were fearful of other birds and animals, especially monkeys. It also took them a while to get used to perching on moving branches—in captivity, their perches were all fixed. In time, though, they became accustomed to their new surroundings—so comfortable that they are now breeding in the wild. In September 2004, the first pair of juvenile birds was spotted flying with the captive-bred flock.

Captive-bred scarlet macaws sometimes have trouble adjusting to life in the wild, but eventually become accustomed to other animals.

The great green macaws aren't doing as well, however. Margot estimates there are fewer than 50 in the wild in Costa Rica. The caged-bird trade has taken its toll, and the species of tree they like to nest in has been extensively logged. The tree is now officially protected and people have begun replanting them, but they mature slowly and it will take time for them to recover.

In the meantime, Richard and Margot are encouraging great green macaws to breed in captivity. "Maybe soon we'll be able to make a release," says Richard. He's confident the birds will survive even without their preferred tree, since the birds can learn to find new nesting locations. "Our green macaws nest in 40-gallon metal drums."

What can people do to help these macaws? "Don't buy a bird without a closed identity ring on its leg," says Richard. "A closed band is considered proof that a bird is captive-bred, not taken from the wild."

TRACKING RAINFOREST BIRDS

P icture a bright green parrot with tinges of muted blue on its head and the back of its neck. Sure, the mealy parrot (*Amazona farinosa*) has a slash of scarlet on its wings and the tip of its tail is pure yellow, but that doesn't make the mostly green bird any easier to spot 50 feet above the forest floor in the dense foliage.

That's why scientists like Robin Bjork, who spent three years studying the parrot, use special devices to track rainforest birds. Bjork attached radio collars to 21 parrots in Guatemala. By flying above the trees, holding up an antenna that picked up the signals emitted by the collars, she could track their movements.

But not all scientists have access to expensive radio collars and small airplanes. Bjork was lucky. Most scientists have to track birds using only their sharp ears, a sturdy pair of boots and good binoculars. Sometimes they set up fine nets to capture birds, attach small metal bands around their legs, and release them. Recapturing the banded birds later allows the scientists to accumulate information about their movements.

∧ Scientists will sometimes climb 100 feet into the rainforest canopy to look for birds.

For the most part, people who study birds spend days, weeks, even months under the forest canopy, listening for the calls of particular birds and recording their movements and behavior. But don't feel too sorry for them. They're passionate about the birds they study and committed to learning as much as they can in order to better protect them. And they get help from a growing army of amateur birdwatchers who share that passion.

∧ A field researcher holds a mealy parrot that he has just radio-tagged to track its movements.

51

The yellow-crested cockatoo (*Cacatua sulphurea*) is a magnificent bird—all white except for a long, forward-curling yellow crest, two yellow ear patches, and a bit of yellow under its wings and tail. "They are beautiful and fascinating birds," says Stuart Marsden, a biologist at England's Manchester Metropolitan University who has studied the effects of forest loss and the caged-bird trade on cockatoos in Indonesia. "They live a long time, learn lots, and seem to look after each other."

But looking after each other hasn't been enough to keep the bird off the critically endangered list. It's just too attractive for its own good. For many years, the yellow-crested cockatoo was one of the world's most popular caged birds, a relatively inexpensive pet until the mid-1970s, when people began to worry about the number being traded. In 1981, it was protected by CITES, though trade continued—between 1981 and 1992 almost 100,000 cockatoos were exported from Indonesia.

"With so many cockatoos being captured from the wild, it is vitally important that the birds reproduce successfully to replace the birds the trappers are taking," says Marsden. "So we set up a study to examine the cockatoo's nesting habitats."

The beauty and charm of the yellow-crested cockatoo have led to it becoming one of the most popular caged birds in the world.

THE FUTURE FOR RAINFOREST BIRDS

There is growing awareness that every bird matters, from the small and beautiful banded cotinga to the magnificent harpy eagle. But it will take more than awareness to avoid the extinction of hundreds of species of rainforest bird.

What do these birds need to survive? Rainforest, for one thing. Preserving what remains should be the first priority. Scientists must also learn as much as they can about these complex ecosystems and the birds that live in them. Conservationists will need to work together with governments and local people to determine which forests should be preserved to ensure the least loss of species.

With enough information, it's possible that selective logging and the extraction of gas, oil, and minerals from some areas could be carried out in a sustainable way. Developing countries might also promote ecotourism—with people paying to view the birds in their natural habitat—as a way of earning money.

Rather than growing single crops in large areas of cleared rainforest, farmers can plant small patches of different crops, some in the shelter of the forest canopy, providing a wider range of habitats for rainforest birds. Stopping the trade in endangered birds would also go a long way towards protecting rainforest species.

But none of these things can happen without addressing the poverty in countries where these birds live. As long as governments are crushed by big debts, they will continue to see rainforests as a quick source of income. As long as people have no choice but to graze their cattle in the forest or trap birds to survive, these practices will continue. And rainforests will remain under siege as long as people in wealthier countries buy exotic pets and consume wood products, coffee and beef with no thought to their real cost to the planet.

The future is in our hands.

< A family group of red-and-green macaws in flight in Tambopata National Park, Peru.

FAST FACTS

^ Double-wattled
cassowary

Scientific names	• there are approximately 9,500 bird species, making up 195 families in the mammal class Aves
Size	• the smallest rainforest bird, the bee hummingbird, is 2.5 inches (6.3 cm) long and weighs less than 0.1 ounces (3 g)
	• the largest rainforest bird, the double-wattled cassowary, grows to almost 6 feet (2 m) and can weigh 130 pounds (60 kg)
Life span	• smaller birds live three to five years in the wild; larger species can live 40 to 50 years
Locomotion	• forelimbs are adapted for flight, with feathers and lightweight bones
	• small birds can fly short distances at 10 to 20 miles per hour (16 to 32 kph); larger species can fly long distances at 40 to 60 miles per hour (65 to 100 kph)
	• also get around by swimming, walking and hopping
	• some bird species have lost their power of flight; others are so adapted to the water that they are helpless on land
Senses and communication	• birds have keen vision, but their sense of smell is not highly developed
	• birds communicate by engaging in sometimes elaborate displays, such as raising and shaking their feathers or bobbing their heads, which can be either threatening or friendly
	• songs and other sounds establish territory, attract mates, keep birds together and express alarm; young birds use begging calls to stimulate their parents to feed them

Reproduction • most birds build nests, where they lay one to 20 eggs

• they sit on their eggs to incubate them, which can take 11 to 80 days

• some birds are nearly naked and helpless when they hatch; others hatch with a heavy coat of down

• some birds are independent almost as soon as they hatch; others may spend more than 200 days in and around the nest

Diet • many birds eat insects and have developed many techniques for catching them: flying with their mouths open, snatching them from the air, digging them out of crevices and from under the bark of trees, licking them out of anthills and pecking them from leaves and other vegetation

• some birds are carnivorous, and have developed long talons and hooked bills for capturing and tearing into the flesh of other animals

• many birds feed on seeds, fruit and nectar

INDEX

PHOTO CREDITS

AUTHOR'S NOTE

This book is dedicated with love to my niece Anna Kenyon-Evans.

One of the great pleasures of writing this book was working with people around the world who share a passion for and dedication to birds. I am particularly grateful to Richard Thomas of BirdLife International in the UK for so graciously answering my questions and introducing me to experts far and wide.

Thanks also to Bennett Hennessey, Jonathan Barnard, Somprat Polchoo, Petch Manopawitr, Joe Foy, Neva Murtha, Christian Boix, Mike Weston, Rachel Bristol, Richard and Margot Frisius, Brian Sykes, Jeni Shannaz, Steve Parr, and Stuart Marsden.

I am most grateful to Dan Bortolotti, whose skillful editing greatly improved this book. Special thanks to Lyle Friesen of Canadian Wildlife Service, for sharing his expertise and for inspiring my love of birds in the first place, and to Myra Friesen Weaver for reviewing the manuscript and providing helpful feedback.

And the most special thanks of all to Christopher Hatton for his steady support and encouragement from start to finish, and for taking me places where rainforest birds live.